NATURAL
DISASTERS

Tim Wood

Wayland

TITLES IN THIS SERIES

AIR DISASTERS

ENVIRONMENTAL DISASTERS

NATURAL DISASTERS

SEA DISASTERS

Cover

(Background) Many millions of people each year are affected by famine because drought-stricken land cannot support livestock or grow crops.
(Inset) Natural disasters come in many forms such as earthquakes, floods and forest fires which can destroy thousands of hectares of land and put many lives in danger.

Series editor: Geraldine Purcell
Series designer: Helen White

© Copyright 1993 Wayland (Publishers) Ltd

First published in 1993 by Wayland (Publishers) Limited
61 Western Road, Hove, East Sussex, BN3 IJD, England

British Library Cataloguing in Publication Data
Wood, Tim
Natural Disasters. – (World's Disasters Series)
I. Title II. Jackson, Tony III. Series
363.3

ISBN 0-7502-0848-1

DTP by Jenny Searle
Printed and bound by G. Canale & C.S.p.A., Turin.

CONTENTS

NATURE'S FORCES UNLEASHED

Earthquakes, volcanic eruptions, floods and hurricanes are all natural events. They only become disasters when they have terrible effects on people. The destructive power of an earthquake or a hurricane both fascinates and horrifies us. Natural disasters remind us all that humans have little defence against the gigantic natural forces that constantly change and shape our planet.

BELOW Each year, massive areas of the world's tropical rainforests are destroyed. This deforestation can lead to soil erosion, landslides and floods.

STRIPPING THE EARTH

The conditions that turn a natural event into a disaster are often created by humans themselves. Cutting down trees for building materials or clearing land for farming, strips away the natural vegetation that keeps soil in place. Heavy rainfall in these deforested areas can wash away soil, making floods worse and causing landslides.

OPPOSITE Kilaueau volcano in Hawaii erupting, throwing red-hot lava 200 metres into the air. The Hawaiian islands have many active volcanoes.

The Earth and the air above it are warmed by the Sun – the heat then escapes slowly into space. Many people believe that pollution from factories and motor cars builds up in the air and does not let all the heat escape. This steady increase in the world's temperatures is called global warming. One danger connected to the problem of global warming is that the world's ice sheets in the polar regions could melt and this would raise sea-levels across the world. Higher sea-levels would increase the danger of flooding in low-lying areas. Some scientists believe that unless we work to try to stop global warming, up to half of Bangladesh could be underwater by the year 2030.

Natural disasters are almost always worse in developing countries which cannot afford to build defences to save more people and property. These countries do not usually have good television or radio networks which could warn people in danger areas, nor modern transport systems which could move people away from danger quickly and safely.

When a disaster does strike a developing country, the loss of life is much greater because most of the people live in flimsy houses. People are more likely to lose their homes and to die from starvation or disease, which so often follow a natural disaster.

You may wonder why these people do not move away from the danger areas. Usually,

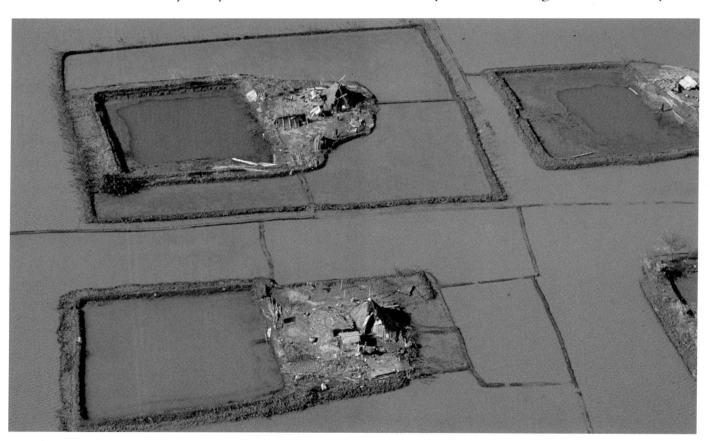

ABOVE *Farms cut off by floods in Bangladesh – one of the countries worst affected by rising sea-levels and deforestation.*

NATURAL DISASTER TABLE

TYPE OF DISASTER	% DEATHS
• Floods	39
• Hurricanes, typhoons and cyclones	36
• Earthquakes	13
• Volcanic eruptions	2
• Tornadoes	1
• Landslides and avalanches	1
• Other (including forest fires, storms, snowstorms, heatwaves).	8

the reason is that many of the developing countries in the world are also overpopulated (too many people living in particular areas). This means that people have no choice but to live in areas where there is always the danger of rivers bursting their banks, landslides, volcanoes erupting or other natural events. There is simply nowhere safer for them to go.

AFTER THE EVENT

A developing country will also take much longer to recover from a disaster, because its government will not have the equipment and vehicles to set up a major relief operation. The roads are likely to be built badly, so help will take longer to arrive.

International relief efforts may help to deal with immediate problems but often natural disasters have long-term effects. Many years after the rest of the world has forgotten the event, the victims will still be struggling to pick up the pieces of their shattered lives.

BELOW Villagers on Sandwhip Island, Bangladesh, try to clean up after a cyclone in 1991.

WHEN THE EARTH EXPLODES

Volcanoes are openings in the crust of the Earth through which gas and molten (liquid) rock escape. Volcanoes have been responsible for some of the most spectacular natural disasters in history. One of the great dangers of a volcano is that it can be unpredictable. It may lie dormant (inactive) for hundreds of years, appearing to be completely extinct (dead). People may live on its slopes, farming the rich volcanic soil, without giving the nearby mountain a moment's thought.

Under the ground, the main outlet or 'vent' of the volcano may be blocked by a plug of solid lava which makes the pressure build up until the volcano blows itself apart with a massive explosion.

A volcanic eruption is a spectacular sight. Often, red-hot lava shoots out of the volcano in a fiery fountain and pours down the side setting fire to everything in its path. Sometimes a volcano can erupt with such force that it destroys itself – covering a large area with rocks and ash. Most deaths from volcanic eruptions are caused by people being smothered in ash or volcanic mud, poisoned by gas or drowned by a tsunami (a large sea wave caused by an underwater earthquake or volcanic eruption). Often, those who survive the immediate dangers later die of starvation because crops and livestock have been destroyed.

LEFT This eruption of the volcano, Stromboli, on the island of Sicily, in 1972, showered the surrounding land with red-hot ash and lava bombs.

POMPEII IS LOST

One of the most famous eruptions in history occurred in AD 79 when the volcano Mount Vesuvius, in Italy, erupted. It destroyed the nearby Roman towns of Pompeii and Herculaneum, burying the houses and more than 20,000 people under ash and mud.

FAMOUS ERUPTIONS

(AD 79) Mount Vesuvius, Italy: 20,000 people in the towns of Herculaneum and Pompeii buried under ash and mud.

(1669) Mount Etna, Sicily, Italy: 20,000 people killed in earthquakes which accompanied the eruption.

(1783) Mount Laki, Iceland: 10,000 people killed by poisonous gas, and famine which followed the eruption.

(1792) Mount Unzen, Kyushu, Japan: 10,000 people killed.

(1815) Tambora, Sumbawa, Indonesia: 90,000 people killed by tsunami and famine.

(1883) Krakatoa, Indonesia: 36,400 people killed by tsunami.

(1902) Mount Pelée, Martinique: 30,000 people killed by hot ash and poisonous gas.

(1919) Kelud, Java, Indonesia: 5,500 people killed by mud flow.

(1980) Mount St Helens, USA: 60 people killed by hot ash.

(1985) Nevada del Ruiz, Colombia: 22,000 people killed by mud flow.

(1986) Lake Nyos, Cameroon: 1,700 people killed by a giant bubble of poisonous gas from the lake which had formed in the crater of the volcano.

ABOVE *The ancient city of Pompeii, now cleared of the ash which buried it, has become a major tourist attraction.*

THE GREATEST ERUPTION – TAMBORA, INDONESIA (1815)

This was the largest volcanic eruption in history. About 200 cubic kilometres of ash and rock were hurled into the sky and blown around the Earth – darkening the sky and changing the weather all over the world. In the USA, the following year, 1816, was sometimes called 'eighteen hundred and froze to death' because of extraordinary weather changes, including snow falling in mid-summer.

KRAKATOA – THE BIG BANG

One of the most famous volcanic eruptions was that of the destruction of Krakatoa in 1883.

Krakatoa was a small island off the coast of Sumatra in Indonesia. The island was made up of the peaks of three dormant volcanoes. The volcanoes had not erupted for over 200 years, but inside them massive forces were building up. The first signs of the disaster to come were a series of small explosions and a large column of ash and steam which towered over the island. On the morning of 27 August 1883, the island exploded, blowing itself to pieces with the force of an atomic bomb. The noise, the loudest sound in modern history, was heard 5,000 kilometres away in Australia!

Lava which reached temperatures of over 1,000°C, and balls of red-hot, sticky material called lava bombs, rained down on the surrounding sea. A giant cloud of ash was hurled into the air – darkening the skies for hundreds of kilometres in every direction. The eruption caused a series of enormous tsunamis that were over 35 metres high. These giant waves swamped nearby islands, washing away hundreds of villages and drowning at least 36,380 people.

BELOW This rare photograph, taken from a hillside on a neighbouring island, shows Krakatoa exploding.

RIGHT A cross-section of a volcano.

CRATER

CRUST

MOLTEN ROCK

MAGMA CHAMBER

HOT ASH

ASH FALL

HOT
MOLTEN
LAVA

MAIN
VENT

ROCK STRATA

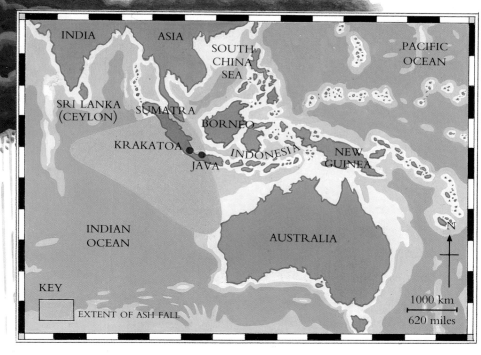

ABOVE A map showing the area affected by the explosion of Krakatoa in 1883.

Within the map:

INDIA

ASIA

SOUTH
CHINA
SEA

PACIFIC
OCEAN

SRI LANKA
(CEYLON)

SUMATRA

BORNEO

KRAKATOA

INDONESIA

NEW
GUINEA

JAVA

INDIAN
OCEAN

AUSTRALIA

N

KEY

EXTENT OF ASH FALL

1000 km

620 miles

WITNESS REPORT

KRAKATOA'S GIANT WAVES

Eyewitness report by Mr N van Sandick, an engineer
on board the ship *Loudon* which was sailing off the
coast of Sumatra:

*'Suddenly we saw a gigantic wave…advancing…with
considerable speed…the ship had just enough time to meet
with the wave from the front…we were lifted up with a dizzy
rapidity…and immediately afterwards we felt as though we
had plunged into the abyss…another three waves of colossal
size appeared. And before our eyes this terrifying upheaval of
the sea…consumed in one instant the ruin of the town; the
lighthouse fell in one piece, and all the houses of the town
were swept away…There, where a few moments ago lived the
town of Telok Betong, was nothing but the open sea.'*
Source: *Krakatoa* by Rupert Furneaux (Published by
Martin Secker and Warburg Ltd, 1965).

MOUNT PELÉE

At 7.49 am on 8 May 1902, the people of the town of St Pierre in Martinique were starting a new day. All of the 30,000 inhabitants must have heard loud explosions as Mount Pelée, the volcano which lay just over 9 kilometres to the north-east, blew itself apart – but only two of them lived to tell the tale. A glowing cloud of gases and red-hot ash burst out of the volcano and shot down the slopes at over 240 kph. The fiery blast, called a *nuée ardente*, lasted only three or four minutes but it shrivelled, smothered or set fire to everything it touched. The only two survivors in St Pierre were a shoemaker, and a murderer who was locked up in the town's jail.

WITNESS REPORT

MOUNT PELÉE DESTROYS ST PIERRE

Eyewitness report by Assistant Purser Thomson, an officer on the ship *Roraima* sailing near Martinique:

'I saw St Pierre destroyed. The city was blotted out by one great flash of fire...As we approached St Pierre, we could distinguish the rolling and leaping of red flames that belched from the mountain in huge volumes and gushed into the sky. Enormous clouds of black smoke hung over the volcano... There was a constant muffled roar. There was a tremendous explosion about 7.45 am ...The mountain was blown to pieces. There

RIGHT This photograph shows the ruins of the town of St Pierre after the eruption of Mount Pelée. Everything in the area was destroyed by fire and only two people survived the disaster.

LEFT This photograph shows the cloud of gases and hot ash, called a nuée ardente, *pouring out of Mount Pelée just before the eruption in 1902.*

was no warning. The side of the volcano was ripped out and there was hurled straight toward us a solid wall of flame. It sounded like a thousand cannons. The wave of fire was on us and over us like a flash of lightning. It was like a hurricane of fire. I saw it strike the cable steamship Grappler *broadside on, and capsize her. From end to end she burst into flames and then sank. The fire rolled in a mass straight down on St Pierre…The town vanished before our eyes.'*

Source: *Volcanoes* by K Wilcoxson (Published by Cassell, 1967).

PREDICTING AN ERUPTION

It is not possible to stop volcanoes erupting, so scientists concentrate on studying them and trying to predict when they could become dangerous. The scientists who study volcanoes are called volcanologists.

Using special heat-proof clothing, volcanologists sample the lava and take measurements with sensitive instruments such as lasers. When magma pushes up from inside the volcano it can cause the sides to bulge. Volcanologists measure these bulges with machines called tiltmeters. There are often small earthquakes before an eruption which can be recorded by special machines called seismometers. Volcanologists have had some success in predicting eruptions using these methods. When an eruption does take place, lava flows which threaten houses can be redirected with explosives and dikes built from concrete and lava. When Mount Etna, in Italy, erupted in April 1992 all these methods were used to prevent the lava flow from smothering the surrounding villages.

RIGHT During Mount Etna's eruptions in 1992, barriers were built, using mechanical diggers, to protect houses and redirect the lava.

EARTHQUAKE!

Earthquakes are caused by movements which occur at the edges of the giant plates which make up the Earth's crust. These plates float on the hot, molten rock of the mantle below and are constantly on the move. As one plate slides past another, the rocks at the edges of the plates grind together. Sometimes the plates do not move smoothly and the two edges stick together until, with a great jerk, they snap past each other. This sudden release of energy causes an earthquake. Shock waves, called seismic waves, spread outwards from the centre of the earthquake – called the epicentre. The deeper the epicentre, the further the shock waves travel, causing damage over a wide area.

EARTHQUAKE – CHILE (1960)

Chile, in South America, experiences frequent earthquakes. In 1903, 3,000 people were killed and in 1939, 40,000 people died. The city of Concepción has been destroyed five times by earthquakes.

In June 1960 the most violent earthquake in modern times hit Chile, killing 5,700 people and making over 1 million people homeless. The earthquake's epicentre was at Concepción – it measured 8.5 on the Richter scale. The tremors, or earth movements, shook down buildings, trapping hundreds of people in the ruins. Huge cracks appeared in the ground. The earthquake triggered landslides and avalanches in the surrounding areas.

LEFT Rescue workers looking for survivors pick through the rubble of buildings after an earthquake in Mexico City in 1985.
BELOW A child is carried away to safety.

Although thousands of people were killed by the tremors and the damage they caused, more died as a result of the after-effects of the earthquake. Roads, railways and bridges were twisted or ripped apart, leaving stricken areas cut off from help. In remote places hundreds of people died from their injuries as they lay crushed or trapped under the rubble before rescue workers could arrive.

In many towns and villages, underground electricity cables and gas pipes were split open – creating fires which raged through shattered houses.

Reservoirs and lakes burst open, and water pipes were broken. The damage to the water supply made fighting the fires even more difficult. Sewage leaked into the damaged water system, leading to the outbreak of serious diseases, such as cholera and typhoid, in some places.

In many areas the land sank several metres. This massive shift of land created a series of tsunamis which hit many coastal towns, drowning thousands of people. For several days, extra-high tides washed over the ruins of ports and seaside resorts.

━ WITNESS REPORT ━

CHILE (1960) – THE EARTHQUAKE BEGAN IN SILENCE

One newspaper reporter, Patrick O'Donovan, described the destruction he saw:

'The earth movements began in utter silence. There was no warning subterranean (underground) rumble. And then came the long-drawn-out appalling noise of wrecking, of tearing and falling and a continuous silly tinkle of breaking glass. Sometimes fissures (cracks) opened in the ground wavering for 100 metres in parallel ripples, imitating the waves on the sea-shore. And when it was all over the birds began to sing very loudly. And then there were fires.'

Source: *Daily Telegraph*, 7 June 1960.

RIGHT After the earthquake in Chile, in 1960, even those houses left standing were so badly damaged that they had to be demolished.

WHERE EARTHQUAKES HAPPEN

Almost all the world's major earthquakes occur at the edges of the plates which make up the surface of the Earth. More than three-quarters of them occur at the edges of the Pacific plate. This area is sometimes called the 'Ring of Fire'. Most of the other earthquakes occur above the plate edges which stretch across Asia from Burma to southern Europe and North Africa. Areas such as Japan, Indonesia, and the countries which lie on the west coast of the Americas are especially vulnerable to earthquakes.

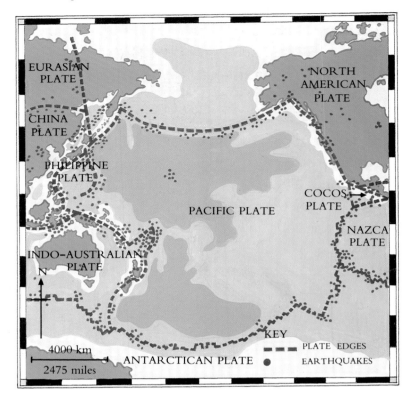

ABOVE RIGHT A map showing where earthquakes have struck around the Pacific plate area.
RIGHT A seismograph measures earth tremors.

EARTHQUAKE PRECAUTIONS

Although scientists constantly monitor movements of the Earth's crust with sensitive instruments, such as seismometers, they are not yet able to predict exactly when or where an earthquake is going to happen. Those areas that are hit most often by earthquakes have to prepare for the worst. Tokyo, in Japan, and San Francisco, in the USA, have both suffered major earthquakes in the past. These cities have been rebuilt to avoid further large-scale destruction.

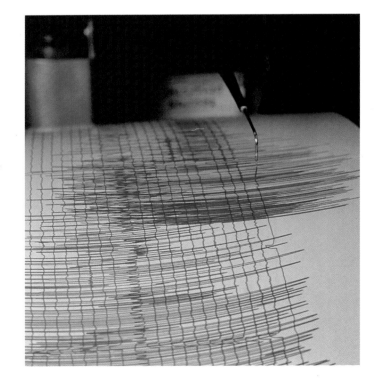

In Tokyo there are strict regulations controlling the size and design of buildings as well as the materials used. 'Quake-proof' tanks of water and stockpiles of food and blankets have been prepared throughout the city.

The wide streets of San Francisco are designed to allow buildings to sway without crashing into each other. The wide streets would also help prevent the spread of fire after an earthquake. Some buildings have very deep, or even sprung, foundations to withstand the shock waves and tremors.

Even in underdeveloped countries, such as Iran and Armenia, houses in earthquake areas are now built with special reinforcements.

Other precautions include protected gas and water pipes and electricity cables. Skilled teams of firefighters and rescue workers have been trained to respond to a disaster. They use heat-seeking instruments that can pick up the body heat of survivors buried under collapsed buildings.

LEFT *Many buildings in San Francisco are built to withstand earthquakes. The wide foundations and base of the Transamerica building make it much more stable when there are earth movements.*

THE ARMENIAN EARTHQUAKE

On 7 December 1988, Armenia (at that time a republic of the former USSR) was struck by one of the strongest earthquakes ever recorded. Worst hit was the large town of Spitak, which was completely destroyed. It was estimated that over 55,000 people died during the disaster.

Armenia is a remote and underdeveloped country. Lack of equipment such as bulldozers and cranes made rescue attempts almost impossible.

500,000 people were made homeless – with only tents for shelter against the harsh winter weather. After their plight was reported on television and in newspapers around the world international relief workers began to arrive to help in the stricken area.

ABOVE In 1923, an earthquake almost totally destroyed the Japanese capital, Tokyo. The earthquake killed 140,000 people and made 1.5 million people homeless.

RIGHT Rescue workers shifting the rubble of collapsed buildings after the 1988 earthquake in Armenia.

FAMOUS EARTHQUAKES

(1201) Syria: possibly the earthquake which caused the largest loss of life in human history. An estimated 1 million people died.

(1556) Shensi Province, China: an estimated 850,000 people died.

(1896) Honshu, Japan: a tsunami 30 metres high and travelling at several hundred kilometres an hour caused by an underwater earthquake in the Pacific Ocean drowned 26,000 people.

(1906) San Francisco, USA: most of the city was destroyed by fire which followed the earthquake.

(1923) Tokyo, Japan: probably the most destructive earthquake in modern times, measuring 8.3 on the Richter scale. In this heavily populated city, 140,000 people were killed and more than 575,000 homes were destroyed. The damage caused was estimated to be over £1 billion.

(1960) Concepción, Chile: the most violent earthquake in modern times, which measured 8.5 on the Richter scale and killed more than 5,700 people.

(1976) Tangshan, China: the earthquake which probably caused the greatest loss of human life in modern times. It measured 7.8 on the Richter scale and resulted in at least 240,000 deaths, although some estimates put the death-toll as high as 500,000, many of them as a result of famine and disease which followed.

(1988) Spitak, Armenia: 55,000 people were killed and 500,000 people made homeless.

AVALANCHE!

BELOW Once many tonnes of snow and ice have been set in motion it is almost impossible to control or predict the course of a major avalanche.

An avalanche is a mass of ice and snow which breaks away from the side of a mountain and falls at great speed. Avalanches often occur in springtime as the ice and snow on the sides of mountains begin to melt. The most dangerous type is called a 'dry-snow' avalanche. An avalanche of this type is made up of dry, powdery snow which can form an icy cloud hundreds of metres high. This huge cloud of snow and ice races

down the mountainside at a speed of over 300 kph. Avalanches can be triggered off by any disturbance, such as strong winds, the movements of a skier, or by loud noises.

In 1916, during the First World War, about 18,000 Italian and Austrian soldiers, fighting in the Dolomite Mountains in northern Italy, were killed by over 100 avalanches, which were triggered off by gunfire.

MOUNT HUASCARAN AVALANCHE – PERU

The single most destructive avalanche in history occurred in 1970 in Peru. The avalanche began when 1 million cubic metres of snow was shaken off a glacier on the western side of Mount Huascarán by an earthquake. The huge, freezing mass fell 3,000 metres and crashed into the slopes below, setting off another 24 million cubic metres of ice and snow. As the avalanche raced down the mountain it picked up rocks, trees, earth and other debris.

The gigantic mass roared into the valley below at 400 kph, engulfing the towns of Yungay and Ranrahirca – flattening buildings as if they were made of paper. About 30,000 people were killed – buried under ice, snow, rocks and mud. The only survivors in Yungay were a few people who managed to run to safety in the town's cemetery!

Rescue work was made more difficult by the bad weather which followed. With roads buried under the snow and mud, the only way into the disaster area was by helicopter. Low cloud and rain stopped the helicopters

ABOVE This aerial photograph shows how the avalanche from Mount Huascarán swept away the town of Yungay, Peru. The circled area shows a high area of ground where some survivors were found.

landing for several days. The first rescuers to reach the stricken towns were 100 soldiers who parachuted through the clouds.

AVALANCHE DEFENCES

Many different methods are used to reduce the danger of avalanches. Sometimes explosives are used to release large masses of snow before they become dangerous.

In some known danger areas avalanche fences are put up and trees are planted to slow down or redirect moving snow. Roads and railways are protected by concrete tunnels. Some ski slopes are closed during the avalanche season to prevent accidents.

SEA OF MUD – THE ARMERO LANDSLIDE

The town of Armero in Colombia, South America, lay high in the Andes mountains in a valley which was overlooked by the volcano, Nevado del Ruiz. The snow-capped volcano had been dormant for over 150 years when, in 1985, it began to stir. A series of minor eruptions, which hurled rock and ash over several kilometres, made the people of the area uneasy. But few could have guessed at the horror to come.

On 13 November 1985, the volcano began to shudder. Scientists who had been watching the volcano sent out a warning to the town of Armero, but for some reason very few of the people moved away.

Just before midnight, two loud explosions in the distance woke many of the townspeople. Some rushed to the town square. Others just went back to sleep. Unknown to them, high above the town, the heat of the volcano was melting its ice-cap. An enormous mass of water, rocks, mud and fallen trees began to slide down the slopes of the volcano. The massive landslide took about two hours to arrive at Armero.

BELOW A sea of mud around the town of Armero. Only the highest ground escaped being smothered by the landslide.

ABOVE An eruption from the volcano Nevado del Ruiz set off the landslide which destroyed Armero.

BELOW The mud flow buried or tossed aside everything and everybody in its path.

WITNESS REPORT

WALL OF MUD

Newspaper reporter, Robert Tyler was at Armero at the time of the disaster. Eighteen months later he wrote the following description of the scene:

'The wall of mud and water was 150 feet (50 metres) high when it slammed into the panic-stricken town in the black of night. Evacuation had begun, but too late. The horrific deluge engulfed 23,000 people, sweeping many of them away as they fled to high ground…It was impossible to tell whether the humps in this slime were cattle or bodies. But the tractors the wrong way up, the one solitary lorry the right way up, all swept higgledy-piggledy across the land, show that no human being caught in the mud's grip could survive.'

Source: *Sunday Times*, 14 June 1987.

The landslide claimed 21,005 victims in Armero. The town and an area of 36 square kilometres around it were buried under 15 metres of mud. The rescue operation was a nightmare. The mud was too soft to bear the weight of the rescuers or their heavy equipment. The only possible way of rescuing the victims was by helicopter.

Most of the trapped people who survived were pulled from the mud within the first three or four days. By the time international rescue teams arrived, few victims were still alive. Not many people could survive more than a few days partly buried in mud, injured and without food. Bodies of the victims continued to rise from the depths of the mud for at least two years after the disaster.

Most of the survivors now live in a new town nearby which was built by the government. Every one of them lost a relative or friend in the disaster. Even so, because the mud could be turned into fertile farmland, it is probably only a matter of time before some begin to move back to Armero.

LANDSLIDE!
The worst landslide disaster in history occurred in Kansu Province, China, in 1920. About 180,000 people were killed by a series of landslides which were triggered off by a single earthquake.

ABOVE *This dazed and mud-caked elderly man was one of the survivors of the disaster at Armero, Colombia.*

OPPOSITE *Rescuers struggled to save this child who had been trapped in the freezing mud for two days. Sadly, the child died before he could be pulled free.*

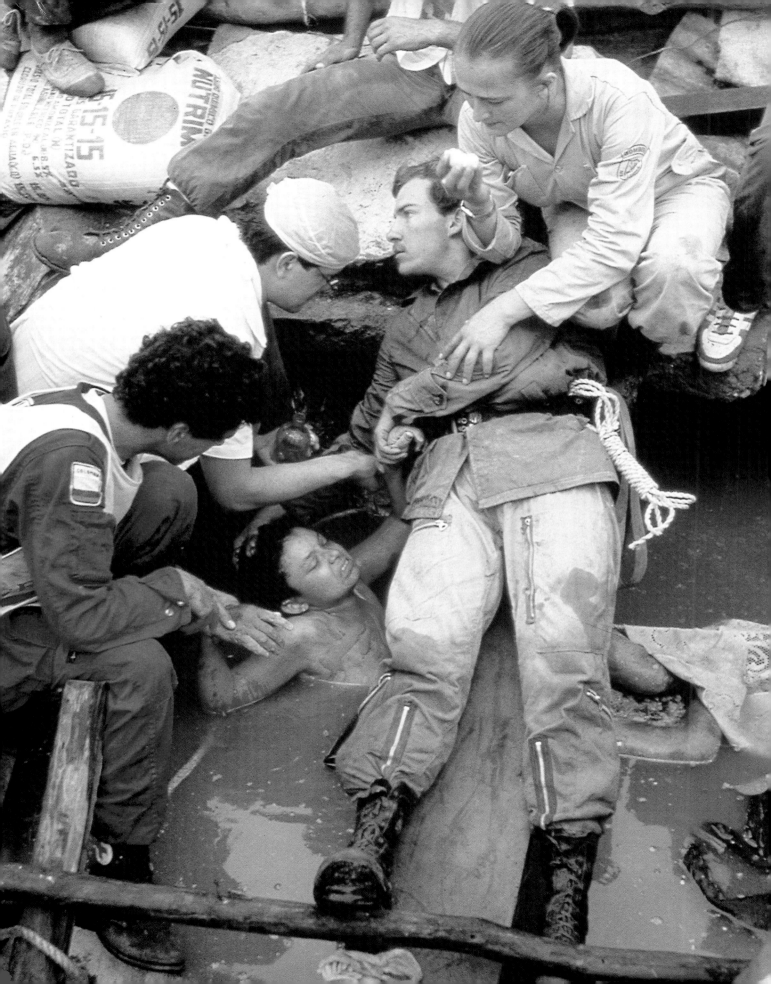

THE EYE OF THE STORM
– HURRICANES

Violent, spinning storms – called hurricanes in the Caribbean, typhoons in the China Seas, and cyclones in the Indian Ocean – are probably the most destructive of all natural events.

The storms begin over warm seas. The sea heats the air above it which rises swiftly, sucking in colder air below. The heated air spirals upwards, gathering moisture and creating towering thunderclouds.

ABOVE A photograph taken from space of a typhoon travelling across the Pacific Ocean.

The storm, which can be up to 2,000 kilometres across, begins to spin faster and faster and, driven by the wind, starts to move over the surface of the Earth at speeds up to 50 kph. At the centre of the storm is a calm area, known as the eye. In a circle immediately around the eye, the winds can reach speeds of 200 kph.

As a hurricane moves across the sea it whips up huge waves which can reach heights of up to 25 metres, creating a terrifying hazard to ships. As the storm approaches the land these waves, often up to 10 metres high at this time, begin to break over the shore. This is called a storm surge. The surge floods the land behind and destroys buildings and fields. It is the storm surge which usually claims most victims.

BELOW A map of northern Australia showing the route of Cyclone Tracy.

STORM WARNING – DARWIN DESTROYED

Throughout Christmas Eve, 24 December 1974, warnings about the approach of a cyclone were broadcast on television and radio over northern Australia.

Few people in the port town of Darwin in the Northern Territory took much notice. They were busy getting ready for the celebrations the next day and believed, or hoped, that the cyclone would pass them by.

At 1.30 am on 25 December, Christmas morning, *Cyclone Tracy* hit the town with the violence of an atomic bomb. Winds of up to 240 kph smashed through the town, destroying over 90 per cent of the buildings in about four hours. At least forty-five people were killed and 10,000 homes were destroyed.

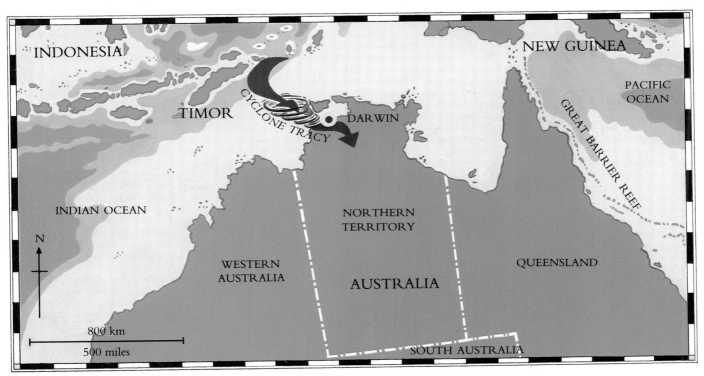

CITY WEATHER
Cloudy periods.
Est. max., 25C.
Yesterday's temperatures:
Min., 11.5C; max., 20C.
December 25 last year:
Min., 17.8C; max., 27C.
Weather Map, Page 55.

The Advertiser

Incorporating "The Register"

Family
Forum,
Page 41

ABS
FOR BRAKES

Television, Page 45

Vol. 117, No. 36,237   56 Pages 8c   ADELAIDE THURSDAY, DECEMBER 26, 1974   Phone 51 0421, Classified only 51 0261

49 dead:
more likely

30,000 people
homeless

All supplies
of power cut

Food short,
no fresh water

CYCLONE FLATTENS DARWIN

CYCLONE TRACY
DIRECTLY ABOVE
DARWIN

BRISBANE

PERTH

ADELAIDE

SYDNEY

MELBOURNE

A satellite picture showing cyclone Tracy centred over Darwin. It was taken from the Esso-8 satellite from 1,200 kilometres (745

City smashed to

At least 49 people are dead and hundreds more were injured in a cyclone which devastated Darwin yesterday.

The death toll could reach more than 100 as rescuers pick their way through a city almost obliterated by the nightmare 180 kph (100 mph) winds.

Officials say up to 30,000 people are homeless. Power is cut. There is no fresh water. Food is short.

Ninety-five p.c. of the city's buildings have been destroyed or mauled by the bombardment.

All communications were cut soon after the cyclone struck early yesterday.

Makeshift refugee camps have been set up to look after the thousands of homeless people.

An airport official at Katherine, 320 kilometres (200 miles) south-east of Darwin, said early today cars were already arriving in Katherine from Darwin.

He said more than 20,000 might have to be evacuated.

He had seen pictures of the disaster and "they are not a pretty sight."

People were in a state of shock.

Planes were already flying into Darwin but they were "going in blind."

There was no power or communication and the Darwin airport was using portable flares.

The planes were being directed from Katherine.

The official said the Darwin airport runway had been cleared but there was still debris on the taxiways.

The management of the Pine Tree Motel at Katherine (Mrs. C. David) said: "All accommodation has been taken and they are opening the hospital and school for them."

The only communications from Darwin have been through a WA ship anchored in the harbour.

Overseas Telecommunications officials from Darwin are sending Morse-code messages and using a one-way radio-telephone from the ship to communicate with OTC in Sydney.

All telephone and telegram links with Darwin are cut.

VIP aircraft carrying the director-general of the National Disasters Association (Maj.-Gen. A B. Stretton) and the Minister for Northern Development (Dr. Patterson) arrived in Darwin last night.

An RAAF Hercules was also on the way to Darwin from the Richmond, NSW, air base with a medical team and equipment.

The Darwin hospital, police station and post office were all virtually destroyed by the cyclone.

Fannie Bay gaol, the city's museum, the Victoria Hotel and Chinese temple are among landmarks reported wrecked.

Officials said many people were killed when they tried to drive away from their houses in the wake of the cyclone.

Many cars were thrown from the roads by the winds.

The Minister for Defence (Mr. Barnard) has put the whole of the defence forces at the disposal of Maj.-Gen. Stretton.

The Navy has ordered crews of the HMAS Melbourne, Brisbane and Stuart to return to their ships and be ready to sail to Darwin today.

The Melbourne will take helicopters and other general supplies.

Melbourne detectives drive British Labor MP Mr. John Stonehouse (centre) to the Federal detention centre in Melbourne yesterday.

Runaway MP
wants to stay

From our Staff Representative

MELBOURNE — The runaway British Labor MP, Mr. John Stonehouse, who was arrested in Melbourne on Tuesday, wants to remain in Australia.

His Melbourne solicitor (Mr. J. A. Patterson) said yesterday: "Mr. Stonehouse will make approaches to stay in Australia.

"He has been detained on a passport irregularity. There is no suggestion of any criminal charge being laid here or in WA."

Three changes to
England Test side

ABOVE The report in this Australian newspaper described how Cyclone Tracy struck Darwin.

The cyclone simply flattened the town. Houses, mainly made of corrugated iron and boarding, were torn from their foundations and battered into pieces. Parked cars were blown over. Railway engines and carriages were tossed about like toys. Telegraph poles were knocked over.

Several people were killed as the cars in which they were driving were plucked off the road by the cyclone and turned over. Others were crushed as their houses collapsed around them. Several people were hit by flying debris and jagged pieces of glass.

The twenty-seven ships in the harbour moved out into open water to ride out the cyclone. Only six returned – some disappeared and others were driven ashore. One ship was picked up by the wind and blown 200 metres inland.

Bob Hedditch, the skipper of the prawn trawler *Anson*, had to lie on the floor of the wheelhouse as his boat rode out the cyclone. It was his engineer's first trip to sea. When the trawler returned to dock, the engineer left the ship and never went to sea again.

Most people hid in the rubble of their homes while the cyclone howled around their ears. Two-year-old Katherine Ginis spent six hours lying in a bathtub sheltered by her father while their home fell apart around them. At Darwin Airport, fifty aeroplanes were destroyed on the ground. Heavy rain added to the chaos, and to the misery of the victims.

The town was left with no electricity, water, fresh food or working sewers. The government, fearing that typhoid and other diseases would break out, arranged for 36,000 people to be flown to safety. Police patrolled the town, ready to shoot any looters and thieves. After the people had left, the familiar sounds of the town disappeared. The silence was eerie. The dogs and cats were shot to save them from a slow death from starvation. Even the birds left.

Compared with other areas which have been hit by strong winds, Darwin was lucky. Although the damage was estimated at AUS $250 million, few people died. The town was rebuilt and the new buildings were designed to stand up to cyclones. The walls were made stronger to guard against the impact of flying debris.

BELOW Darwin was totally rebuilt after the destruction caused by Cyclone Tracy. The new buildings have been designed to withstand the terrible storms that form across the ocean.

WITNESS REPORT

CYCLONE DESTRUCTION

This is how the scene after the cyclone was described by Gareth Parry, a reporter.

'Darwin resembled a matchbox town crushed by a giant foot. Streets were littered with trees, smashed cars that had been picked up like pieces of paper and hurled for hundreds of metres, and the rubble of destroyed buildings.' Source: *The Guardian* ©, 26 December 1974.

RIGHT Most of the buildings in Darwin were totally destroyed.

FOLLOWING A HURRICANE

Nothing can be done to stop a hurricane, cyclone or typhoon. Instead, meteorologists try to identify them and plot their paths. Satellites in space take photographs of the Earth which are used to spot a hurricane forming. Aeroplanes with special equipment on board fly round the fringes of a hurricane measuring its strength and plotting its course. Weather stations throughout the world exchange information and use computers to work out the likely direction of the storm.

All this information is used to warn people who live in the path of a hurricane, so they can be moved out before the disaster occurs. However, this is not always successful. If the predictions are wrong the hurricane may take a different course and strike somewhere else.

Sometimes, as in Darwin in 1974, people do not listen to the warnings or there is not enough time for people to leave the area.

ABOVE A meteorologist studying images from a US weather satellite.

CYCLONE DANGER FOR BANGLADESH

One of the main ways to reduce the damage done by cyclones is to build stronger houses with storm-proof basements and strong shutters to protect the windows.

In developing countries it is not possible to build millions of new homes. Bangladesh has solved this problem by building dozens of large cyclone shelters. These are rather like wartime air raid shelters. Each is designed to hold about 1,500 people but can hold more than three times this number in a real emergency.

The cyclone shelters are raised 4 metres above the ground so the people inside will be safe from the storm surge flooding which usually follows a cyclone in this low-lying country.

In November 1970, between 500,000 and 1 million people were killed by a cyclone that hit a group of islands off the coast. Less than half the islanders survived.

In developed countries, towns situated near the sea are protected from a storm surge by strengthened sea defences.

BELOW The home of this Bangladeshi family has been destroyed by a cyclone.

LEFT Workers in Bangladesh building a cyclone shelter. The vertical steel rods are to reinforce the concrete of the walls.

HURRICANE HAZARD – *HURRICANE ANDREW*, USA (1992).

Hurricanes are named alphabetically. The first of the season is given a name beginning with A, the next one B, and so on. The names are male and female in turn.

In August 1992, *Hurricane Andrew* swept across the South Atlantic and struck Florida, USA with all of its might.

Leaving a trail of destruction in its wake, the hurricane moved on across the Gulf of Mexico and hit the coast of Texas.

BELOW Hurricane Andrew *left a trail of devastation in its wake.*

TORNADO!

Tornadoes are violent, twisting storms. They are like hurricanes but are smaller, more powerful and they move much faster. A tornado will usually form over land, in warm, moist air, where winds blow into each other from opposite directions. These winds create a spinning funnel of wind, inside which hot air rises at great speed. The funnel tightens to form a whirling column about 50 metres across. The wind in this column can reach speeds of up to 300 kph and the tornado can race across the ground at speeds of up to 100 kph. As it travels the tornado sucks up dust and debris and the howling wind can smash the walls of the strongest buildings. Tornadoes can snatch up cars, aeroplanes and even railway engines, and hurl them into the air as if they were toys.

As it passes over the land, the low pressure area inside the tornado creates a vacuum, causing buildings to explode as the windows are sucked outwards. Anyone caught directly in the path of a tornado has little chance of survival.

BELOW The whirling, funnel-shaped cloud of a tornado touching down in the Midwest of the USA.

WATERSPOUTS

Waterspouts are tornadoes which occur at sea. The whirling column of the storm picks up water from the sea and also contains rainwater from the clouds above. However, waterspouts are much weaker than tornadoes and last only a few minutes.

THE 'PALM SUNDAY TORNADO OUTBREAK'

Tornadoes form in many parts of the world, but they are most frequent and most violent in the flat, central areas of North America.

RIGHT A rare photograph of a waterspout. Usually, they form for only a few minutes.
BELOW A map of North America showing the Tornado Alley area.

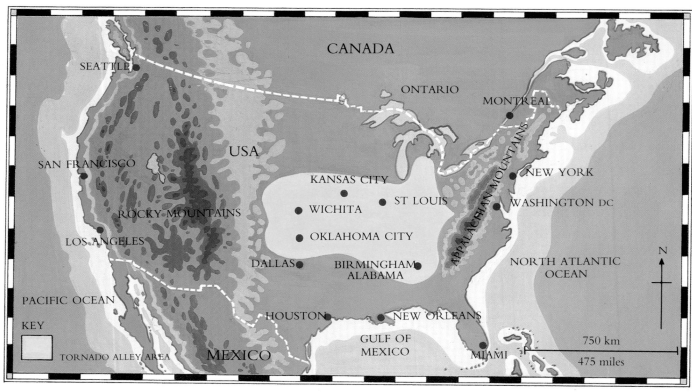

ABOVE This photograph shows a tornado travelling across Oklahoma, USA in 1965.

Parts of Kansas, Oklahoma and Missouri in the USA are called 'Tornado Alley', because as many as 700 tornadoes form there every year. Most of these tornadoes last less than ten minutes and travel at no more than 50 kph. However, there is good evidence to suggest that winds inside certain 'super tornadoes' have reached speeds of over 1,000 kph. This is very hard to prove because scientific instruments which might measure the speeds accurately are always destroyed by the tornado!

Tornadoes often occur in groups called swarms. One of the worst swarms in American history, called the 'Palm Sunday Tornado Outbreak', happened on 11 April 1965. In the space of nine hours, thirty-seven tornadoes formed in six separate states in the USA. A total of 271 people were killed. One of the tornadoes lifted an entire farmhouse 18 metres into the air!

The worst year for tornadoes in the USA was 1925, when 700 people were killed throughout the Tornado Alley area.

A GIANT SWARM OF TORNADOES

One of the most intense periods of tornado strikes in North America was in April 1974. Within the space of eight days, 100 tornadoes formed – racing across the landscape, cutting a path of destruction from Alabama in the south to Ontario in Canada. A total of 324 people were killed and 4,000 more people were injured. Some were killed by sand and gravel, which had been sucked up by the tornadoes, striking them like bullets. Some were torn to pieces or hit by flying objects. Others were stabbed by wheat straws that sliced into them like darts. After the tornadoes, such straws were found driven deep into the trunks of trees.

Although many people had been killed, some luckier people and animals were lifted by the tornado and put down some distance away, totally unharmed.

Two of the worst hit towns were Xenia, Ohio and Brandenburg, Kentucky. Brandenburg was a small farming town of 1,600 people. The town had never experienced a tornado before and its inhabitants were totally unprepared for the disaster. In a five minute strike a tornado smashed through the town, killing twenty-nine people and injuring many more. Most of the dead were children who had been playing outside their school. Three-quarters of the buildings were destroyed. Eyewitnesses spoke of cars, people and even houses flying through the air. The disaster ripped the heart out of the small community and many of the survivors left, never to return.

BELOW This town in Kentucky, USA, was badly damaged during a tornado strike.

WITNESS REPORT

XENIA, OHIO – TARGET OF A TORNADO

When the swarm of tornadoes hit Xenia, Ohio, half the houses were destroyed, twenty-eight people were killed and nearly 600 injured.

Many shops in the town were totally destroyed. One shopkeeper, William Mitchcock, standing outside his jewellery shop described the strike.

'"It hit at 4:40," he said, looking up at *the clock in his twisted shop sign. The hands were frozen at 4:40 pm.*

"We close on Wednesday afternoon…so I was away from the store at the time, but it passed just a little south of our home. It sounded like a fast passenger train. It was really just filling the air with stuff, really violent." '

Source: *New York Times*, 5 April 1974.

ABOVE *A shop destroyed by a tornado strike.*

XENIA – A TOWN IN SHOCK

A reporter described another scene:

'The storm cut a swatch a half-mile (one kilometre) *wide and three miles* (five kilometres) *long through Xenia – all in five minutes. One terrified elderly victim, the roof of her small frame house completely blown away, sat wrapped in a blanket in a rocking chair…When firemen tried to persuade her to leave, she simply shook her head, refusing to say a word.'*

Source: *Time Magazine*, 15 April 1974.

PROTECTION FROM TORNADOES

It is impossible to predict the exact time and location of a tornado strike because the whirlwinds move so fast and can change direction unexpectedly. Meteorologists track tornadoes with radar scanners and issue warnings to areas which may be in danger.

There is no real protection from a tornado. People directly in its path have little hope. Most buildings in areas which are likely to be struck are usually built with strong cellars. When a tornado is in the area the people go into the cellars and hope that the tornado will not pass directly over them.

There have been many powerful tornadoes in the Far East. They are particularly destructive in India and Bangladesh, where millions of people live in flimsy houses with no cellars. These countries also lack good emergency services and this means more people are put at risk. The worst tornado disaster occurred in Shaturia, Bangladesh, in 1989 when 1,300 people were killed in a single strike.

CUMULONIMBUS CLOUD

FUNNEL

PATH OF TORNADO

ABOVE A diagram to show how a tornado forms. BELOW Fragile houses in Bangladesh are especially vulnerable to cyclones and tornadoes.

THE MIGHT OF FLOODS

There are many different causes of floods. The most usual is a period of heavy rain or melting snow and ice which causes rivers to rise and burst their banks. In coastal areas unusually high tides added to strong winds can cause the sea to flood on to land. Storm surges created by hurricanes and tsunamis caused by earthquakes or volcanic eruptions, can also lead to disastrous floods.

The collapse of a dam can result in great loss of life. In 1963, the Vaiont Dam in Italy burst and the flood that followed killed more than 1,800 people.

FLOOD IN HONDURAS

On the night of 18 September 1974, *Hurricane Fifi* hit Honduras in Central America.

Although warnings had been given, thousands of people who lived in remote areas of the country either had not heard the warnings or were unable to leave. In thirty-six hours 60 centimetres of rain fell.

BELOW This couple's house in Honduras was destroyed totally when Hurricane Fifi *hit the area in 1974.*

In the mountains, the streams and rivers began to overflow. Banks and dikes burst, and the muddy, brown waters poured on to the land. Thousands of houses and hundreds of the most fertile fields were swept away. Dirt roads, railways and bridges were washed away, cutting off many areas from help.

The town of Choloma was worst hit. Buildings were carried off and over 3,000 people and many thousands of animals drowned. Worst hit were the old and the young who quickly became exhausted when they were swept away by the flood water. The Honduran army collected the bodies, piled them in great heaps and burned them. It was important to dispose of the bodies quickly to stop diseases spreading.

The flood waters carried mud and other materials that poisoned the wells and rivers which supplied the drinking water. Honduras is a poor country with few helicopters, boats and other emergency vehicles. Many of the worst-hit areas were

RIGHT Survivors from Choloma crossing a flooded valley.

remote, so rescue work was hard to organize. A huge international relief effort had to be launched. The final death-toll throughout the country was 8,000, with another 400,000 left homeless.

A GRUESOME DISCOVERY

When the flood subsided the dazed survivors discovered that the whole area was covered with a 3-metre thick layer of mud. Roads, bridges and railways had disappeared. Bodies lay everywhere.

One survivor, who had lost his entire family, returned to the wreckage of his home and discovered the bodies of two complete strangers there. He said they were *'just poor innocents who were swept down the mountain and ended up here'*.

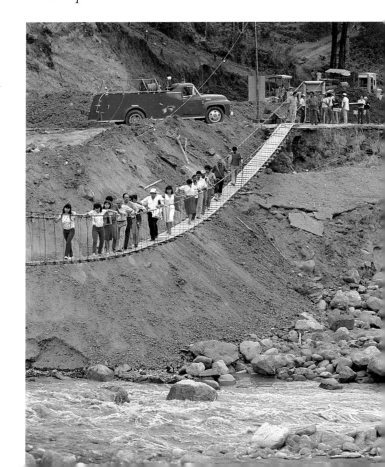

'CHINA'S SORROW'

Most floods are caused by rivers bursting their banks. The Hwang Ho or Yellow River in China is the greatest disaster area on Earth. Over the last 3,500 years it has flooded more than 1,500 times and has taken more lives than any other natural feature in the world. This has earned the river the nickname of 'China's sorrow'. In 1887, one of the greatest flood disasters in history killed nearly a million people when the Yellow River burst its banks.

The reason for these disastrous floods is that the river flows along a channel which is 3 – 6 metres above the surrounding land. The rise of this channel is partly caused by the efforts of people to stop flooding. They have built giant dikes of earth, reinforced with bundles of roots from a plant called kaoling, to hold back the river.

Unfortunately, silt (fine soil) is carried by the water and drops to the riverbed. Gradually the silt fills the channel and the water-level rises. This forces people to build their dikes even higher. Over the centuries the riverbed has gradually risen above the surrounding land. This means that when the river does burst its banks, millions of litres of water can flood an area as large as Britain.

CHINA'S OTHER SORROWS

China has suffered several even greater flood disasters. The higher death-tolls are a result of the starvation which has followed the destruction of crops.

In 1931, over 3.5 million people died when the Yangtze River burst its banks.

In 1959, over 2 million people died in North China as a result of massive flooding which destroyed the rice crop.

RIGHT Floods in China in 1931. The townspeople of Hankow had to wade and row through the streets.

BANGLADESH IN DANGER

The low-lying country of Bangladesh is often affected by flooding.

About 40 per cent of the country is no more than 1 metre above sea-level and disastrous floods often follow the cyclones which regularly hit the coast or occur when the rivers Ganges or Brahmaputra burst their banks as a result of heavy rain in the mountains to the north. Bangladesh has experienced five major floods in recent years. The worst was in 1970 when 200,000 people were killed by the tidal surge following a cyclone. The floods which occurred in 1988, when both the Ganges and the Brahmaputra rivers burst their banks, affected about 45 million people directly. Over 30 million were made homeless and 2 million tonnes of food crops were lost. At least 3,000 people were drowned and over 100,000 caught diseases from poisoned drinking water after the flood.

BELOW A map of Bangladesh showing the many islands and low-lying land which are badly affected by floods when the rivers overflow or sea-levels rise.

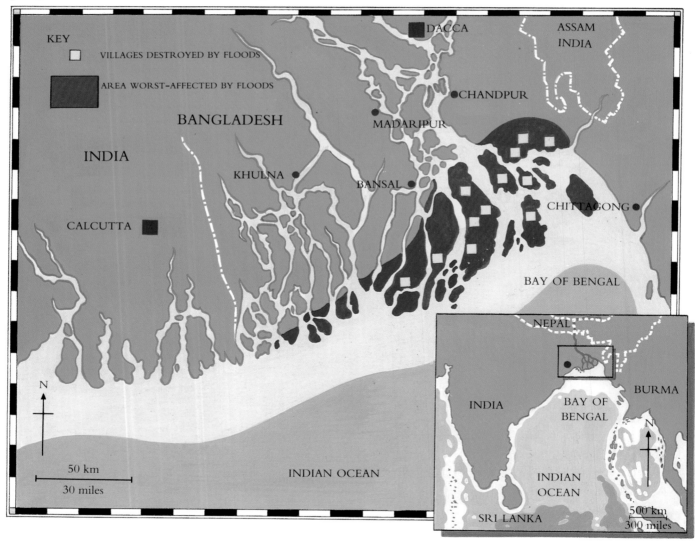

BELOW *These children are carrying jugs of precious fresh water on their heads.*
After a flood, pollution and the diseases it brings often lead to thousands of deaths.

LEFT Fields and villages on an island off the coast of Bangladesh which were flooded by the sea in 1991.

HOLDING BACK THE FLOODS

Flooding can never be stopped completely but constant monitoring of rainfall and river levels by meteorologists in many countries can help to give early warnings of flooding to places which are in danger.

The most important guard against flood for countries at risk from the sea, such as Bangladesh, is better sea defences. Unfortunately, building these defences would be too expensive for a developing country. So, perhaps the only answer is international aid from developed countries.

More long-term measures, such as reducing the use of fossil fuels, would reduce global warming and could stop the slow rise of the sea.

DANGERS OF NATURE

There will always be natural disasters. The forces which cause natural disasters, such as the weather, the sea and activity in the Earth's crust, are much too powerful for human beings to control. In the short term, the best we can do is improve how we monitor danger areas to give early warnings, build better transport systems to move people out of danger more quickly, and keep well-equipped teams at the ready to launch rescues and give relief. In the longer term we must reduce the damage we do to the environment and improve living standards. Only by doing these things can we reduce the terrible human suffering caused by natural disasters.

GLOSSARY

Atomic bomb One of the most powerful and destructive weapons ever developed.

Cholera An infection that causes very bad diarrhoea and can lead to death. The usual cause of cholera is drinking dirty water.

Crust The solid outer surface of the Earth.

Deforested The area of a forest or rainforest that has been cleared of trees.

Dikes Long embankments of earth or concrete.

Famine A great scarcity of food in an area or a country.

Fertile Able to produce a large amount of crops.

Glacier A slow-moving mass of ice and snow.

Lava Molten (liquid) rock that flows at the Earth's surface. This is the substance that flows out of a volcano.

Magma Molten (liquid) rock beneath the Earth's surface, or crust.

Mantle The part of the Earth that lies between the core, or centre, of the Earth and the surface crust.

Meteorologists People who study weather conditions.

Monitor To keep a record, control or check on something, such as the behaviour of a volcano.

Nuée ardente A red-hot cloud of gas and volcanic ash.

Remote A place that is difficult to get to or is out of the way.

Richter scale A mathematical scale (from 0 to 10) which is used to measure the size of an earthquake.

Satellites Machines in space that travel around the Earth. They are used to collect information and send it around the world.

Seismometers The instruments used to measure the force of an earthquake.

Tiltmetres The machines used to measure any earth movement on the surface slope of a volcano.

Typhoid A bad fever caused by drinking dirty water.

Unpredictable When something changes its behaviour without warning.

Vacuum An empty space that has no air or gas.

FURTHER READING

The Destruction of Pompeii by Mike Rosen, (Wayland, 1987)
Earthquakes and Volcanoes by Sara Steel (A&C Black, 1982)
The Eruption of Krakatoa by Rupert Matthews, (Wayland, 1988)

Flood by Brian Knapp (Macmillan, 1989)
The Violent Earth series (Wayland, 1992)
Volcanoes and Earthquakes by Basil Booth, (Wayland, 1988)

PICTURE ACKNOWLEDGEMENTS
Camera Press Ltd 15, 34 (top) (Hoflinger), 38; Explorer 8 (K Krafft), 22 (K Krafft), 23 (both) (K Krafft), 40 (bottom) (K Krafft); Frank Lane Picture Agency 30 (top), 35 (W Carlson), 36 (R Steinau); John Frost Historical Newspaper Services 28; Impact Photos Ltd 4 (C Jones), 17 (B E Rybolt), 31 (B Edwards); Photri 32 (bottom) (F Siteman), 33, 37; Popperfoto Ltd 10, 41; Press Association 21; Rex Features Ltd 9, 12 (left), 18 (left) (SIPA), 39 (M Naythons /SIPA), 40 (top) (M Ginies), 44-5 (L Chamussy); Science Photo Library 30 (bottom) (L Migdale); Frank Spooner Pictures 6 (Bartholomew/Liaison), 13 (right) (E Signorelli), 16 (Giboux), 24 (Bouvet/Hires/Duclos), 25 (Bouvet/Hires/Duclos), 32 (top) (P Nucero); Tony Stone Worldwide cover (background) (A Darling), cover (inset) (D Austen); Topham Picture Library 5, 7 (U Weitz), 12-13, 14 (both), 18-19, 26, 43 (P Rahmantstr); ZEFA 20 (N Gillette), 29 (Eugen).

All illustrations are by Tony Jackson.

ACKNOWLEDGEMENTS
Quote on page 37 (bottom): copyright 1974 Time Inc. Reprinted by permission.

INDEX